Trump in the Middle

Why America Needs a Middle Child This Time Around

Heather Collins-Grattan Floyd

ISBN-10: 1535555807
ISBN-13: 978-1535555807

DEDICATION

To my wonderful family:
My husband, Kevin Floyd;
my parents, the Rev. Robert and Ann Collins;
my sister, Heidi Collins;
my parents-in-law, Gene and Carol Lempicki; and
our pit-bull and bichon frisé,
Jigsaw and Ketchup.

CONTENTS

ACKNOWLEDGEMENTS

I'd like to thank all of the people who participated in my marriage-compatibility survey for my book *The Compatibility Matrix: The Qualities of YOUR Ideal Mate*, all of whom answered the question about birth order. Their participation taught me a number of things about this aspect of psychology and family dynamics, and how that part of growing up affects your own personal perspective of the world and your role in it.

PREFACE

When I was in sixth grade, it was 1983, and I'd
already developed an interest in politics. There
were four of us girls who were good friends in
our class at Bancroft Elementary School in
Minneapolis, Minnesota – but when we started
discussing the upcoming presidential election of
Ronald Reagan vs. Walter Mondale (who was a
Minnesotan), we had a horrible argument that
split us two-and-two.

Karen B. and I were Republicans; Karen K.
and Lisa were Democrats. Briefly, the four of us
weren't all speaking to each other! I'm

embarrassed to admit that I'm probably the one who started the argument, because I couldn't see the logic of the opposing side.

Reagan won 49 states except one: Mondale's home state of Minnesota. Frankly, I was glad he won at least one state, because he was a nice guy and I didn't want him to be completely shut out!

So I've been interested in politics at least since the sixth grade.

Fast-forward to the 2000s when I was writing the book *The Compatibility Matrix: The Qualities of YOUR Ideal Mate.* I included a chapter on politics – because the survey found that it indeed is very important that two people be compatible with each other on a political level – and I was very careful to write it in such a way that my readers wouldn't be able to tell what my political perspective is, because that doesn't matter. What does matter is the individual.

I've developed the perspective that God continues to bless the United States by allowing us to have two large parties. Not one, not five, but two. And when one party has been in power for a while, the voters tend to like to toss it to the opposing party for a change of pace. So we generally must decide between two good candidates, and a majority of Americans pray that we have the collective wisdom to cast the correct lot. "Not my will, but Thy will be done." Amen.

THE GIFTS

He wasn't supposed to be here. Donald Trump has been famous for decades for owning large buildings, casinos, and golf courses, as well as for his three marriages and five children. And, of course, for hosting the TV show "The Apprentice," and his trademark line from the show: "You're fired."

Ouch.

Such baggage! So how can he possibly be so massively popular among conservative, traditional, family-oriented people for the presidency?

Because he's genuine, honest, and believable. And most of all, capable.

Still, why have so many Americans been willing to look past his blustery character and storied past to vote for him in 2016?

The Middle-Child Difference

Donald Trump is the fourth of five children: Maryanne, Freddy, Elizabeth, Donald, and Robert, in that order. The oldest son in a family – even if he has older sister(s), as Freddy did – often has firstborn-type traits because he tends to be given leadership roles that demonstrate or utilize his strength.

However, Freddy was never very interested at their father's real estate construction business like his younger brother Donald was. Also, Freddy developed an alcoholism/addiction problem at a fairly young age, and he died of his addiction at age 43. Donald writes in his book, *Trump: The Art of the Deal*:

My older brother, Freddy, the first son, had perhaps the hardest time in our family. My father is a wonderful man, but he is also very much a business guy and strong and tough as hell. My brother was just the opposite. Handsome as could be, he loved parties and had a great, warm personality and a real zest for life. He didn't have an enemy in the world. Naturally, my father very much wanted his oldest son in the business, but unfortunately, business just wasn't for Freddy. He went to work with my father reluctantly, and he never had a feel for real estate. He wasn't the kind of guy who could stand up to a killer contractor or negotiate with a rough supplier. Because my father was so strong, there were inevitably confrontations between the two of them. In most cases, Freddy came out on the short end.

Eventually, it became clear to all of us that it wasn't working, and Freddy went off to pursue what he loved most – flying airplanes. He moved to Florida, became a professional pilot, and flew for TWA. He also loved fishing and boating. Freddy was probably happiest during that period in his life, and yet I can remember saying to him, even though I was eight years younger, 'Come on, Freddy, what are you doing? You're wasting your time.' I regret now that I ever said that.

Perhaps I was just too young to realize that it was irrelevant what my father or I thought about what Freddy was doing. What mattered was that he enjoyed it. Along the way, I think Freddy became discouraged, and he started to drink, and that led to a downward spiral. At the age of forty-three, he died. It's very sad, because he was a wonderful guy who never quite found himself. In many ways he had it all, but the pressures of our particular family were not for him. I only wish I had realized this sooner.

Fortunately for me, I was drawn to business very early, and I was never intimidated by my father, the way most people were. I stood up to him, and he respected that. We had a relationship that was almost businesslike. I sometimes wonder if we'd have gotten along so well if I hadn't been as business-oriented as I am.[1]

THE BIRTH ORDER FACTOR

In this book, I make the argument that Donald Trump has the right personality characteristics for this particular time in history, and a big reason why he exhibits those characteristics is that he was a middle child while growing up.

Almost 70 percent of U.S. presidents have been firstborns (or what I call "virtual firstborns" because their next-oldest sibling is 5 or more years older than they are, so the rivalry is weak) or only-children, which are like super firstborns. Hillary Clinton is a firstborn.

Why Birth Order Matters

Your birth order deeply affects how you perceive your role in relationships with other people. This perception is established at a young age: You quickly learn if your best strategy in getting attention – and getting what you want from your parents – is by being:

- responsible and confident (generally firstborn/only-child traits),
- cute and irresistible (generally lastborn traits), or
- adaptable and bringing everyone together (generally middle-child/twin traits).

In the chapter about birth order in my book *The Compatibility Matrix,* I wrote that middle children are often the best at showing empathy to others and at listening attentively. They also tend to have the least amount of confidence (true inner confidence), because they were outperformed by their older siblings and "out-cuted" by their younger siblings.

Therefore, middle children learn to impress their parents by being agreeable and differentiating themselves from their siblings in that important way. And they tend to be humble, which their close friends and acquaintances always see, but those who don't know them personally may not.

The Most Flexible Birth-Order Type

The middle child is the most versatile of the birth-order types. They're equal-opportunity folks: They can identify with firstborns, because they, too, had younger siblings whom they probably picked on; they can identify with lastborns, because they were probably picked on themselves by their older siblings; and they obviously relate well to fellow middle children.

They can identify the *least* with only-children because, naturally, an only-child is accustomed to being the *center* of attention most of the time – all of the adult eyes are on them – whereas a middle child is accustomed to having to *share* the attention most of the time.

...Compare That to Firstborns

Firstborns typically display a perfect smile at a moment's notice, lots of confidence in whatever they're tasked to do, and a bit of a know-it-all personality. If you watched the first debate between Trump and Hillary Clinton on September 26, 2016, it was almost 2 full hours of Hillary maintaining a knowing, smug grin, and Trump with a serious-looking semi-grimace.

Trump said several times during the debate some variation of "Secretary Clinton and I agree on this," whereas Hillary only said that one time toward the end, when she seemed to feel like she had to bite the bullet and show a small level of agreement. Middle children always strive to bring and/or keep everyone together. Having to argue with Hillary was noticeably hard on him, and I believe that that's because he and Hillary had had a cordial/professional relationship in the past, until they became opponents in this election race. She and her husband Bill (who was president from 1993 to 2000) had even attended Trump's wedding to Melania in Palm Beach, Florida, in January 2005.

...Compare That to Lastborns

Lastborns are the cutie-pies of the world, and parents tend to coax the older siblings into leadership roles. So the leadership style of lastborns is usually friendly, not too dominant.

We're All Friends Here

Being a middle child, Trump rarely displays a wide toothy smile, and even when he does, he closes his lips quickly. And that displays a self-deprecating behavior. He also doesn't fight like a firstborn – while a firstborn is more likely to put their opponent to shame by displaying more intelligence or capability, Trump gets in the mud and calls names, such as "Crooked Hillary."

And this comes across as tongue-in-cheek humor to those who agree with him, and as scathing playground taunts to those who don't.

Middle children tend to feel that they're theglue in the family, and they need to keep the peace between the older siblings and the younger siblings. They thus can argue vehemently in one moment and then switch to "hey, we're all friends here" the next – and that works for them for a lifetime.

We've seen Donald Trump exhibit that very behavior/mentality during this election, as if: Hey, I called you Crooked Hillary, but you came to my wedding, I've supported you in the past, and I'm trying to win an election – so we all know what's going on here – we're all just playing the game.

Toward the beginning of the first debate on September 26, 2016, Trump was answering a question posed by the debate moderator, Lester Holt. Now, much ado had been made in the media beforehand about what Trump might call Hillary during the debate, since he had indeed used some of his scathing nicknames during the Republican primary debates.

Trump looked at Hillary and said, "'Secretary Clinton?'" [Pause.] "Yes?" As if to gain her approval of this reference.

She nodded.

"Okay," he said, "I want you to be happy with me."

So that question was answered, he wouldn't call her "Crooked Hillary" during this debate! Isn't it interesting how he phrased it, "I want you to be happy with me"? Bringing everyone together in that moment.

When have we ever witnessed a presidential candidate say to another presidential candidate, "I want you to be happy with me?" It's very different from what we're used to. The self-deprecation is refreshing for those of us who believe that he's being real.

These relationships and different-than-usual mannerisms all make the game of politics in 2016 absolutely captivating.

HOW TRUMP FINDS COMMONALITY
WITH YOU

In December 2012, I was widowed after being married for almost 19 years. My husband Ron died of GBM (glioblastoma multiforme) brain cancer, that horrible form of primary brain cancer that's very difficult for researchers to study. So I was very interested in donating plenty of money to cancer-research causes, so fewer women would have to be widowed from that insidious disease like I was at age 41.

One of those causes was the M.D. Anderson Cancer Center. In December 2013, I was attending a fundraising gala for M.D. Anderson at Donald and Melania Trump's Mar-a-Lago estate in Palm Beach. I'd heard Donald Trump was there for the event.

Now, I'd already learned that you don't take photos or selfies with famous people you meet on Palm Beach, because pretty much everyone on Palm Beach is either rich or famous, and rich/famous people only like group-photos to be taken by the professional photographer du jour. After all, the rich and famous should be able to have a nice normal life without people ogling over them, right? So if I did run into Trump, I'd decided I was going to treat him with as much normalcy as possible.

My then-boyfriend Jonathan and I were mixing and mingling before the dinner, which is what you do at these events on Palm Beach. First, everyone has drinks, sodas, or Trump Water in that case, and then they ring a bell to let everyone know it's time to enter the gala hall for dinner and, later, dancing.

I was sipping on Sprite when I suddenly realized Donald Trump's back was right in front of me.

Well! You sometimes only get an opportunity like this once in a lifetime.

So I tapped on his back.

He quickly twisted around to face me.

"We love 'The Apprentice!'" I smiled. He grinned back at me. I introduced myself and my boyfriend.

Now, I knew that Donald Trump's parents attended my church at least two times, two Easters in a row, in the early 1990s. Lakeside Presbyterian is located almost directly across the Intracoastal Waterway from Mar-a-Lago, and I knew he'd grown up Presbyterian. So I figured that would be a good thing to bring up.

"My Dad is actually the former pastor of Lakeside Presbyterian Church, right across—" and I motioned with my hand toward the Intracoastal – and he smiled and interrupted:

"Oh! I go there!" he said, as he pointed to

me with his finger.

"Oh!" I said. "Have you been there before?"

Donald sort of hesitated. "I go there!" he said again.

"Well, that's wonderful!" I said in agreement. And then I said something else that I don't remember, because I was truly just enjoying this moment.

He nodded and said, "Have a good time!" with a grin, being very gracious as the owner of this palatial estate, and he turned back to the conversation I'd interrupted in the first place.

The Middle Child's Typical Reaction...

It struck me that he listened to what I was saying to him and immediately made a personal connection with me, not just commentary. Even if he's never stepped foot into Lakeside Presbyterian before himself, he obviously recalled that he had that affiliation to some degree. I was impressed that my church was so top-of-mind to him, because he didn't even hesitate.

Kevin's Turn

I met Trump in 2013, but my husband Kevin met him almost two decades earlier – around late 1992 or early 1993 – when Kevin was the general manager of a local car dealership.

Trump and two large men who looked like bodyguards were walking around the dealership outside. They were all wearing suits, even though it was South Florida and hot as usual.

Kevin was in the showroom when someone said, "Hey, I think that's Donald Trump out there!" Kevin noticed that one of the salesmen was already speaking with Trump outside in front. (Kevin wasn't even sure whether it was really Trump or not until he got a little closer.) So Kevin went out to see if he could be of any assistance.

The brand had recently undergone an image transformation, and the new designs were very impressive. Trump mentioned to Kevin that the new car designs look really good, and he said a few other superficial things.

Kevin had noticed that they hadn't parked in front in the visitors' lot, but must have parked out back. Trump and his two cohorts didn't take a test-drive or anything. Rather, Trump was looking at the intersection area, the perimeter of the property, as well as looking at the cars themselves.

Trump said something to Kevin about how "one of my employees" was looking to buy a car. At that point, the owner of the dealership came over and started speaking to Trump, so Kevin let the two of them talk.

"He does things big," says Kevin, so he thinks Trump was most likely scoping out the property, not looking for a car.

Like Trump says in his book, he loves making deals, especially big deals – and especially when it involves real estate! And when you think about it, making "deals" to help the older and younger siblings get along is exactly what a middle child does.

THE MOST ACCESSIBLE CANDIDATE EVER

One thing about Donald Trump that everyone in the media appreciates is how accessible he's been in this campaign. It's been widely reported that if a media outlet asks him for an interview, he gladly obliges. He prefers to do phone interviews, and they often gladly oblige to that.

One thing everyone loves to talk about is that he tweets. And if some issue is really getting under his skin – usually when Hillary has made an accusation that he says is totally false, but the story is gaining traction – he's known to post something on Twitter in the middle of the night, giving his side of things. Talk about accessible!

He alternates those tweets with warm, kind ones, like this from 10/2/16: "Melania and I extend our warmest greetings to those observing Rosh Hashanah here in the United States, in Israel, and around the world."

Yes, he's becoming a true statesman. This type of tweet will most likely replace any criticism-type tweets if he wins the presidency. As a middle child, he would most likely keep his Twitter feed going, to keep the team together and involved!

From Donald, With Love

Those of us who are on his text-alert list have received some fun texts from him, too. I've listed some of them below; none of them are fixed for spelling or punctuation, just raw, true Donald in his own words, right to your phone!

7/11/16: Folks, I'm getting close to making my VP decision. Click here to make sure you are among the first of my supporters to know: [URL] - Donald

7/19/16: Wisconsin Sheriff David Clarke says "Blue Lives Matter" - If you agree, reply DONATE to make America Safe Again!

7/19/16: We're kicking off Day 2! Donald Trump will #MakeAmericaWorkAgain. Watch our video [URL] and Reply USA for live updates from the convention.

7/20/16: What an amazing night. The Trump-Pence ticket is official and how about my son's speech tonight? Reply back to share your thoughts with me. - Donald

7/23/16: It's been a great night! Mike Pence, our next VP, spoke about how we will Make America First Again. Reply back to tell me your favorite moment! - Donald

8/24/16: I'm looking for 2 dinner guests to join me ASAP! I want to hear your ideas for the campaign. There's not much time. Enter to win now: [URL] -DJT

9/21/16: I need YOUR input today. Only 5 days until I debate Hillary on stage. What do you want me to fight? Tap to let me know: [URL] -DJT

9/22/16: Hey #TrumpTrain, we've only got 47 days to defeat Crooked Hillary. With YOU, we will WIN. Will you commit to volunteer? ARE YOU IN? [URL] -DJT

9/24/16: HUGE OFFER to my biggest supporters-Enter NOW to win a ride aboard Trump Force One w/ me. For a once in a lifetime experience, tap--> [URL] -DTJ (sic)

9/25/16: 1 day before debate & our movement is stronger than ever. Show Hillary just how strong-I need 200k of you to give $1 right now. TAP-> [URL] -DJT

9/26/16: DEBATE DAY! Time for Hillary to face her record. Which failures do you want her to answer for? Vote here--> [URL] –DJT

9/29/16: FINAL FEC deadline is 11:59pm. We're setting records. $20Million goal. Give

today & I'll DOUBLE your donation. Even $1 –
Contribute now: [URL] -DJT

10/1/16: We have just HOURS to go. I need my
strongest supporters to give before 11:59pm to
put us over the top. Don't wait. Contribute
NOW --> [URL] -DJT

Notice that all of these texts listed above
were signed at the end except the second and
third, which must have been written by staff, as
it was the middle of the Republican National
Convention. These are the aspects that strike me
the most:

1)   The tone is as if he's your brother
       speaking with you. He uses "we" and
       "your" a lot, like we're all playing on a
       team together.

2)   Unlike presidential campaigns of the
       past, his communiqués feel very
       grassroots-level. He doesn't try to rise
       above.

3)   He actually makes it fun to donate to

his campaign, asking for even as low as $1.

So you can see, over and over, how his middle-child characteristics shine. He wants to keep everyone together, and he wants to make that personal connection with you. And he's like that naturally across the board in everything he touches.

HOW MIDDLE CHILDREN
FILL A NECESSARY ROLE

Donald Trump understands that his big brother Freddy didn't naturally gravitate toward business. Donald has learned from his experience of Freddy's addiction and death, and he humbly recognizes that Freddy should have been encouraged, rather than discouraged, by the family. You can hear Donald's tenderness and understanding in his writing.

In my book *The Compatibility Matrix*, I wrote that middle children "can blend well with others" and are "great team players." Even though Trump has frequent playground-style brawls with his adversaries, he likes to shake it off and shake hands afterward, and he expects others to have the same forgive-and-forget perspective.

When he began his official career in politics in June 2015, he first resorted to his real-estate-magnate mentality a number of times, acting the same way as if he were dealing with a "rough supplier" or "killer contractor" like usual. So he has had to learn to dial it back. But adjusting is natural for him as a middle child.

Trump's M.O. on TV

Because Donald Trump is a middle child, he doesn't try to outshine the others but rather tries to outperform them.

If you ever watched an episode of "The Apprentice," which he hosted for 14 seasons (including seven seasons of "Celebrity Apprentice") from 2004 to 2016, you saw how he handled the boardroom. Trump, two hand-picked advisors (sometimes his children), and the contestants would all get together in the wood-paneled, dark, intimidating boardroom, and Trump and his two advisors would listen to the contestants talk about their experience in that particular task.

He'd then announce which of the two teams won this task, he'd send out the winning team with his congratulations, and he'd continue the boardroom session with the losing team. Trump would then narrow it down to usually two or three for the final hot seat, and listen to them duke it out. He'd then send them out of the boardroom so he could discuss with his two advisors about who should be fired. At that point, you'd watch Trump spend about one or two minutes collaborating with his advisors.

He always listened attentively to each individual on the show, both advisors and contestants, and he wanted to be fair. But he also wanted to keep the show irresistible to watch, so he wouldn't quickly fire really interesting characters that would keep the viewers tuning in for the next episode!

Now that he's running for president, it's interesting to note that none of his many contestants from the show have come out saying he's a horrible person—even though he fired most of them!

And why might that be?

A Deeper Look

While writing this book, I started to wonder whether Donald really is naturally adept at real estate development, or if he was just motivated to impress his Dad by diving right into it. The answer might be in the very beginning of his *The Art of the Deal* book:

> I don't do it for the money. I've got enough, much more than I'll ever need. I do it to do it. Deals are my art form. Other people paint beautifully on canvas or write wonderful poetry. I like making deals, preferably big deals. That's how I get my kicks.
> Most people are surprised by the way I work. I play it very loose. I don't carry a

briefcase. I try not to schedule too many meetings. I leave my door open. You can't be imaginative or entrepreneurial if you've got too much structure.[2]

So although his detractors focus on his style – his brute personality and aggressive demeanor – they're ignoring the content of his words. And you really can't disparage the content, because he's trying to bring everyone together in pragmatic fashion. Several of his 16 fellow Republican candidates from the campaign have enthusiastically – enthusiastically! – come into the fold of his campaign to help him win, and that's a testimony to his ability to coalesce a team, even among those with huge egos.

Trump sometimes says something and then realizes he phrased it in such a way that it will be misconstrued, so then he makes what seems to be an opposite statement only a few sentences later.

Which drives his opponents nuts!

But as a middle child, he naturally learned to have it both ways. You can beat up and outperform your younger siblings, but you can be beaten up by and outperformed by the older ones. Thus, you learn to adapt and be good at a little of both, and you have to roll with the punches.

And all this might partly explain the dichotomy that puzzles so many people. It's hard to argue with someone who's so quick to agree with you.

WHY SO DIFFERENT?

One reason Trump might be such an enigma is that, at some point while growing up, he stopped seeing his big brother Freddy as the hero of the five siblings, and he realized that he himself was making his father proud as the one who could take over the family business.

So he became the de facto firstborn son of his family, which was ultimately solidified after Freddy's passing when Donald was 35.

And all of this is giving Donald Trump an advantage in this election. He's revolutionary in every way – a unique approach, in-your-face delivery, and focused perspective – which is different than what we're used to in modern times.

Those of us who are in Generation X grew up with the strong, steady confidence of Ronald Reagan as the template of presidential leadership, after having suffered through the years of the Vietnam War and the Watergate scandal. We all watched as Vice President Spiro Agnew resigned amid Watergate, so President Richard Nixon appointed Speaker of the House Gerald Ford to be vice president. When Nixon eventually resigned over Watergate, Ford became president.

And we thought *these* are tumultuous times!

To Be Perfect or Not to Be Perfect

Firstborns innately know that they're expected to be a family leader, and that feeling extends to everything else through their lives – they're basically supposed to be perfect at everything. Middle children like Trump know that they're not perfect at everything, and they don't try to be, but they do try to make everyone happy and bring everyone together.

Firstborns aren't so concerned about bringing people together or making them happy, but rather impressing everyone. And being first. In everything.

These times demand a different set of personal skills and characteristics than we've needed in the past in a president. Because almost all countries have come to question our authority in the world, we need to reestablish our leadership with an unusual blend of nurturing confidence and unrelenting strength.

As a middle child from a highly motivated family, Donald Trump exudes both.

PENCE IN THE MIDDLE, TOO

Trump's vice-presidential nominee Mike Pence, governor of Indiana and a former congressman, is a middle child of six siblings. When you see him smile, it's not a let-me-shine-above-the-crowd smile like a firstborn would, but a somewhat guarded smile like Trump's.

Since being tapped as the VP nominee, he has displayed a much brighter countenance than he has in the past. He used to have a perpetually serious, almost angry look when doing TV interviews – but that look is gone!

A middle child is happiest when they feel

like they're successfully holding everything together, and Pence has been doing just that with aplomb. Whenever he's asked by interviewers about something Donald Trump has recently said, he addresses the rationale behind the comment and makes it sound completely logical, which is of course how Trump intended it to come across.

So Pence a great translator, and he does so naturally as a fellow middle child.

THE CONTENT OF HIS CHARACTER

Trump's supporters are more pro-Trump than they are anti-Hillary. But Hillary Clinton's supporters tend to be more anti-Trump than they are pro-Hillary. This can be easily seen just by watching the evening news these days. They love ranting against Trump, but they have difficulty listing specific actions that Hillary did well as secretary of state or senator. Other than be a woman in that position.

While anti-Trump people tend to judge him solely on his bombast – his style – rather than his content, pro-Trump folks listen to his words and like it. They don't mind the bombast, because they see other countries becoming emboldened by our lack of force and confidence, and they see our values draining away from our culture.

When you feel personally threatened, the ideal protector would be a full-time bodyguard. Trump has that big-man image, combined with a successful businessman's experience, a TV star's persona, and an Ivy League graduate's intellect.

A House Divided – Back Together

Trump likes to say, "This is a movement – it's not about me."

Jerry Falwell, Jr., president of the Christian college Liberty University, said about Trump: "He loves people."

If you'd like to bring America together again, and to experience the successful spirit we've had in the past, it's time to vote for the ticket of the middle child: Trump and Pence.

BIBLIOGRAPHY AND
RECOMMENDED READING

[1 & 2] Excerpts from TRUMP: THE ART OF THE DEAL by Donald Trump, copyright © 1987 by Donald Trump. Used by permission of Random House, an imprint and division of Penguin Random House LLC. All rights reserved.

Trump's book also includes interesting photos of Donald and his family.

ABOUT THE AUTHOR

Heather Collins-Grattan Floyd was the author of *The Compatibility Matrix: The Qualities of YOUR Ideal Mate* (2011). She devised a 3-year Bible-reading plan which was published in the *HCSB Study Bible* (Holman Christian Standard Bible™, Broadman & Holman Publishers, 2010); she was also a contributing writer to *Nelson's New Christian Dictionary* (Thomas Nelson, 2001). She has published articles in Newsmax, the *South Florida Sun-Sentinel*, and *South Florida* and *South Florida Bride* magazines. She was also the editor of "Thy Word Quarterly" newsletter.

Mrs. Floyd holds a bachelor's degree in journalism from the University of Florida, where she was a member of Zeta Tau Alpha sorority and a little sister at Phi Delta Theta fraternity. She is an active elder and deacon in the Presbyterian Church (U.S.A.). She lives in Florida with her husband, Kevin, and their pit-bull and bichon frisé, Jigsaw and Ketchup.

TRUMP IN THE MIDDLE

www.ingramcontent.com/pod-product-compliance
Lightning Source LLC
Chambersburg PA
CBHW060649290526
45793CB00001B/463